The Secret Lives of CATS

VAL and RON LINDAHN

LONGSTREET PRESS, INC.
Atlanta, Georgia

Published by LONGSTREET PRESS, INC.,
a subsidiary of Cox Newspapers,
a subsidiary of Cox Enterprises, Inc.
2140 Newmarket Parkway
Suite 118
Marietta, Georgia 30067

Printed in the United States of America

1st printing, 1996

Library of Congress Catalog Number 95-82231

ISBN: 1-56352-281-0

Jacket and book design by Jill Dible

The Secret Lives of CATS

To our family and friends who encouraged us with this project,
to our cats, Shadow and Sing, who dare to dream,
and to cat lovers everywhere ... enjoy.

Ron Lindahn

☾

To Stutz Bearcat, my friend and pal, who always listened and answered with a
knowing glance of silent feline wisdom. We miss you.

Val Lindahn

CAT O' NINE TALES

Now, a cat that can write is rare thing indeed
while there's many a cat in my town that can read.
The kind of a story they all like to see
has no cat-aclysm or cat-astrophe.

Cats like adventure, the swashbuckling kind,
where the hero must struggle to come from behind.
They like tales of the heart where true love finds her mate,
stands against all odds and tempts her own fate.

Cats like drama, they like fantasy too,
they like plot-twisting mystery and that old derring-do.
They like swords slaying dragons and the magical wish
that instantly changes small boys into fish.

So notice next time that a cat nears a book
(you'll have to be quiet, just sneak a quick look),
see how she smiles, purrs and tosses her head
when she happens to notice a book that she's read.

CONFUSE A CAT

Our cat sees things that just aren't there
(at least not there to you or me),
floating by him in the air,
flighty playmates we can't see.

Flying fish dart through the sky
flashing tail and glistening fin.
He watches as each one goes by-
he'll start to pounce ... then think again.

I've seen him raise a furry paw
(when one should chance to swim too near),
and take a swipe at what he saw
(I still can't see a thing, my dear).

At times he's quite content to sit
and count things floating through the air.
He doesn't seem to mind a bit
that I can't see them; it's just not fair!

CHEAP THRILLS

It's so much fun to be with those
who make us smile and curl our toes.

When Sissy arrives for a leisurely chat,
we lie on the porch on my shaggy brown mat.

Young Harold shows up, sometimes late in the day,
to borrow my toys; I can't get him to stay.

Old Fred is so nice, though his visits are rare,
his wonderful tales make me feel like I'm there.

But to all I confess that it's always a treat
when someone exciting drops by to eat.

KITTY LITTER

Kitty likes to eat and play,
he never puts his things away.
Where he's been is an easy guess,
you won't look far to spot his mess.

So much to do that's not been done
and cleaning up is never fun.
He'd rather stalk, or sleep, or purr,
or roll around, then lick his fur.

He'd rather watch through slitted eye
small motes of dust that pass him by.
Or find a place out of the sun
to lie and nap till day is done.

When he awakes and wants to play,
because his things aren't put away,
he wastes no time, but jumps right in
... of course, he leaves them out again.

SWEET CATOLINE

"Sweet Catoline," four old cats sing their tune,
as the street light above takes the place of the moon.
Old Missus Cartwright who lives 'cross the street
hates those cats singing and stamps both her feet.

Delighting to sing in such sweet harmony
they croon through the night, the one, plus the three.
Old Missus Cartwright proclaims in a shout
that those bad noisy kitties should just cut it out!

As their song echoes far and away down the lane,
cat friends all join them to sing the refrain.
Missus Cartwright claims cat songs she cannot excuse,
so she throws all her dishes, her hats and her shoes.

The cats sing till morning then say their good-byes
and return to their families for custard and pies.
Old Missus Cartwright, all sad and alone,
has nothing to do once the cats have gone home.

PURRPLEXED

(Wish I Had a Nickel)

Cats want most what they can't get.
At times they'll pace or throw a fit,
they'll climb the drapes or claw the couch,
or smack your leg, then grump and grouch.

When they can't have what they think's fair,
they hunker down; for hours they'll stare,
as if by gaze that doesn't falter
they'll cause the circumstance to alter.

SKATING ON THIN MICE

I discovered a new trick,
unbelievably cool.
Don't tell my big brother-
he'll say I'm a fool.
All it took was an iron,
my mom's favorite tool,
some obnoxious rodents
and dad's backyard pool.

You really must try this,
you will feel oh, so nice.
It takes little courage,
you needn't think twice.
Your friends may come join you
when they notice how nice
you swirl and you twirl
as you skate on thin mice.

T.G.I.F.

Thank God it's Fido,
I'm glad he's my friend,
someone I can count on to be there to the end.
When I'm sad he consoles me and says it's OK;
when I'm happy he's frisky, we run, jump and play.

I love when he presses his cold nose to mine,
his ears are all floppy, his eyes seem to shine.
At night he will snuggle to make sure that I'm warm,
and he eases my fear when I'm scared by a storm.

Thank God it's Fido,
he puts me at ease,
I can just be myself without trying to please.
He's my very best friend. Peculiar at that,
to find a dog who is best friends with a cat.

THE ULTIMATE CHEESEBALL

At night our cat will sneak outside
to take his rocket for a ride,
up to the moon, that glistening ball,
away from Earth, the Sun and all.

It's great adventure far away
tracking down pink mice at play,
in holes in craters, all green cheese,
he's master over all he sees.

He loves to pounce and catch a few
just to prove what he can do.
He always lets them go, and then
he tracks and catches them again.

CAT FISH

Cat Fish lazy in the afternoon
when the sun is hot and water cool.
Catfish cruisin' through the deep,
spies a tidbit in his pool.
Cat Fish thinkin' bout days gone by
when summer love would dance and sing.
Catfish thinkin' bout the land above,
home of tasty, wiggly things.
Cat Fish moves his pole a bit,
arranging for a better stance.
Catfish moves in for a bite,
to take it while he has the chance.
Cat Fish caught, quite by surprise,
a monster from the watery deep.
Catfish caught with lightning speed
this savory morsel, his to keep.
So Cat Fish tries hard not to fall
and lose his rod and reel and all.
And *Catfish* tries to spit the bait
or break the line, then hide and wait.
And so each prays to his dear mother,
because, you see, they've caught each other!

FELINE UP

Five cuddly kitties forced to stand in a line,
so the law could tell which one was facing a fine.

That one naughty cat wore a clever disguise
(a fake nose and glasses to cover his eyes).

Then he blamed his poor brother, by using a note,
with hopes he could sneak off to someplace remote.

If truth will be known and justice our wish,
he never intended to break the milk dish.

PURRFECT

When a cat's ninth life is lived and done,
she gets to have an extra one.
First she grows a pair of wings
(they're kind of noisy flappy things),
that let her fly and just have fun.

Climbing rainbows way up high
to jump and glide down through the sky,
then tumbling through a cloudy puff
(rolling in the silvery stuff),
she pounces once again to fly.

So it is with each new day,
a cat's tenth life is spent this way,
joyful rapture overflowing,
confident with inner knowing,
that it's her full-time job to play.

CAT SCAN

Kitty scans the twinkling stars
in hopes of finding life past Mars.
He hopes to find some friends out there,
with alien interests he can share.

He wants so much to find them soon,
he eats his supper beneath the moon.
Through the starry depth he'll peep
till daylight finds him fast asleep.

He's sure that they will have a ship
and lots of time to make the trip.
What a wondrous thing to play
with strange new friends from far away.

KNOCK, KNOCK, WHO'S THERE

Knock, knock. Who's at the door?
What have they come to see me for?
Is it a salesman with shiny black shoes,
with a mission to sell me last week's evening news?
Is it a beggar without a red cent,
looking for handouts to help pay his rent?
Maybe it's Jasper, that old painted mime,
who's come here to spend quiet quality time.

It might be the Ringmaster, Old Circus Joe,
with a pass for tomorrow's elephant show.
Or Old Aunt Mabel, with her bent gnarled cane,
who visits my home to get out of the rain.
I secretly wish it's my old friend the cat,
he keeps me quite safe and I love him for that.
If it's him I'm relieved and I know I'm OK.
If it's anyone else, they can just go away.

Ron and Val Lindahn live deep in the woods of the North Georgia mountains with two cats, Shadow and Sing; their dog, Lady; two birds, Cooter and Amelia; and their son, Sean.

Val has worked as an illustrator for 25 years, bringing magic and a sense of wonder to life through her paintings in books, magazines, posters and movies. In addition to creating award-winning images, Val is an accomplished sculptor, cook and gardener, and is an expert in hairball analysis.

Ron has spent the past 48 years wearing his inner child out. Along the way he has worked as a professional photographer, filmmaker, ski instructor, jeweler, graphic designer, writer, yoga teacher, marketing consultant, illustrator, nail banger and mechanic, and he plays bass guitar with the Atomic Fireballs.

Val and Ron are judges for the international L. Ron Hubbard Illustrators of the Future contest.

If you would like to be correspond with the Lindahns, write

Valhalla Studio
P.O. Box 24
Rabun Gap, GA 30568